PHYSICAL SCIENCE

LIGHT

by Mary Lindeen

NORWOOD HOUSE PRESS

DEAR CAREGIVER, The *Beginning to Read—Read and Discover Science* books provide young readers the opportunity to learn about scientific concepts while simultaneously building early reading skills. Each title corresponds to three of the key domains within the Next Generation Science Standards (NGSS): physical sciences, life sciences, and earth and space sciences.

The NGSS include standards that are comprised of three dimensions: Cross-cutting Concepts, Science and Engineering Practices, and Disciplinary Core Ideas. The texts within the *Read and Discover Science* series focus primarily upon the Disciplinary Core Ideas and Cross-cutting Concepts—helping readers view their world through a scientific lens. They pique a young reader's curiosity and encourage them to inquire and explore. The Connecting Concepts section at the back of each book offers resources to continue that exploration. The reinforcement activities at the back of the book support Science and Engineering Practices—to understand how scientists investigate phenomena in that world.

These easy-to-read informational texts make the scientific concepts accessible to young readers and prompt them to consider the role of science in their world. On one hand, these titles can develop background knowledge for exploring new topics. Alternately, they can be used to investigate, explain, and expand the findings of one's own inquiry. As you read with your child, encourage her or him to "observe"—taking notice of the images and information to formulate both questions and responses about what, how, and why something is happening.

Above all, the most important part of the reading experience is to have fun and enjoy it!

Sincerely,

Shannon Cannon

Shannon Cannon, Ph.D.
Literacy Consultant

Norwood House Press • P.O. Box 316598 • Chicago, Illinois 60631
For more information about Norwood House Press please visit our website at
www.norwoodhousepress.com or call 866-565-2900.
© 2018 Norwood House Press. Beginning-to-Read™ is a trademark of Norwood House Press.
All rights reserved. No part of this book may be reproduced or utilized in any form or by any
means without written permission from the publisher.

Editor: Judy Kentor Schmauss
Designer: Lindaanne Donohoe

Photo Credits:
All photos by Shutterstock

Library of Congress Cataloging-in-Publication Data
Names: Lindeen, Mary, author.
Title: Light / by Mary Lindeen.
Description: Chicago,IL : Norwood House Press, 2017. | Series: A beginning
to read book | Audience: K to grade 3.
Identifiers: LCCN 2017002628 (print) | LCCN 2017019178 (ebook) | ISBN
  9781684041138 (eBook) | ISBN 9781599538815 (library edition : alk. paper)
Subjects: LCSH: Light—Juvenile literature. | Reflection (Optics)—Juvenile literature.
Classification: LCC QC360 (ebook) | LCC QC360 .L5484 2017 (print) | DDC
  535—dc23
LC record available at https://lccn.loc.gov/2017002628

Library ISBN: 978-1-59953-881-5   Paperback ISBN: 978-1-68404-100-8

302N—072017
Manufactured in the United States of America in North Mankato, Minnesota.

Light is all around us.
It is a kind of energy.

Some things make their own light.

The sun's burning gases
make sunlight.

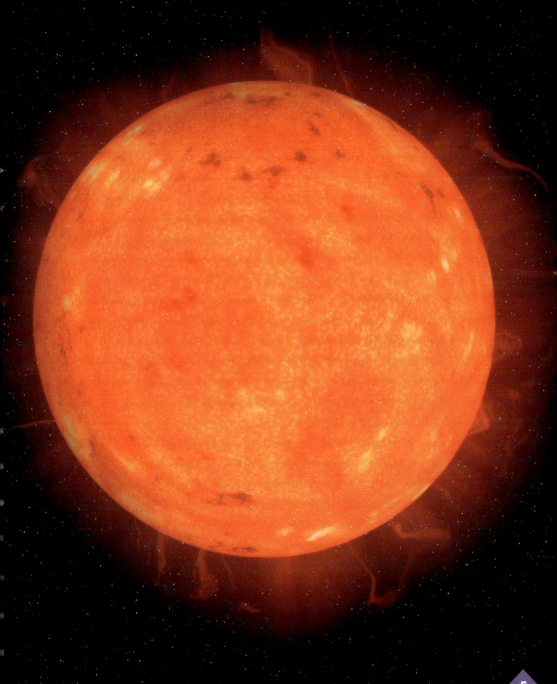

Did You Know?

Something that makes light is luminous. When a flashlight is on, it's luminous.

Glow sticks, fireworks, and light bulbs make their own light, too.

Some living things make their own light.

Fireflies do.

Some mushrooms and sea animals do, too.

The moon doesn't make its own light.

Light from the sun reflects
off of the moon.

That's why we can
see the moon in
a dark sky.

There are many things that don't make their own light.

A book doesn't.

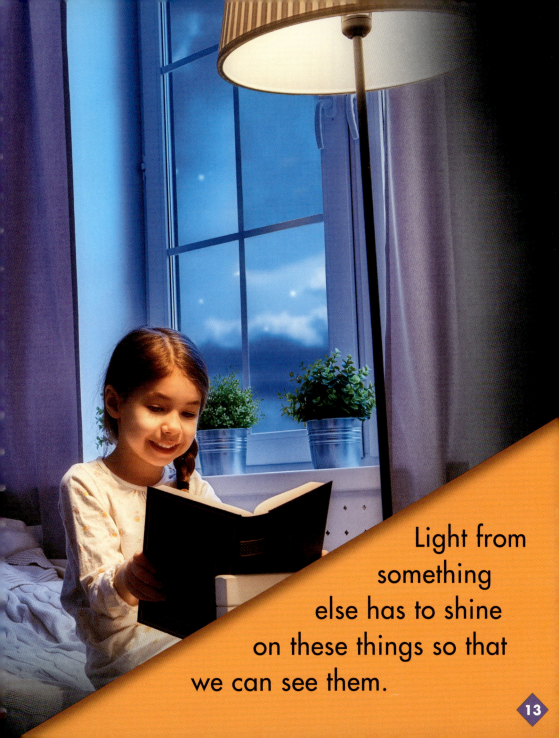

Light from something else has to shine on these things so that we can see them.

Light travels in waves moving so fast we can't see them.

Light waves can easily travel through transparent materials, like glass.

Translucent materials let some light through.

No light can travel through
opaque materials,
like wood.

Light helps us see things.

We can also use light
to communicate.

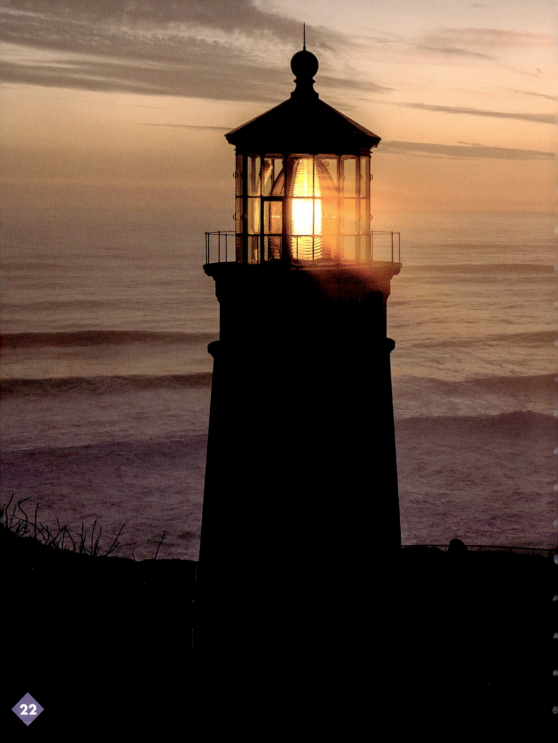

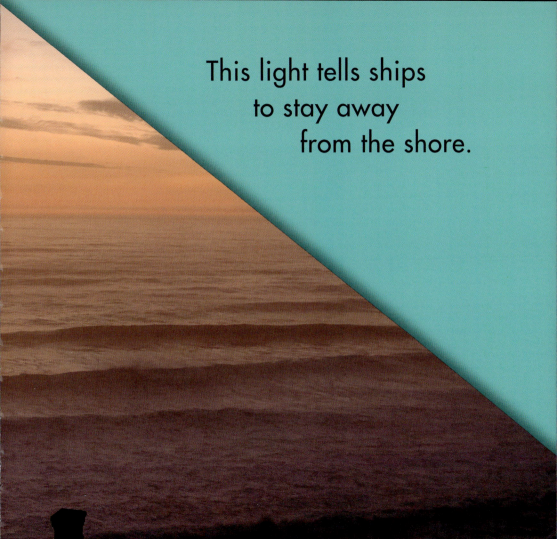

This light tells ships
to stay away
from the shore.

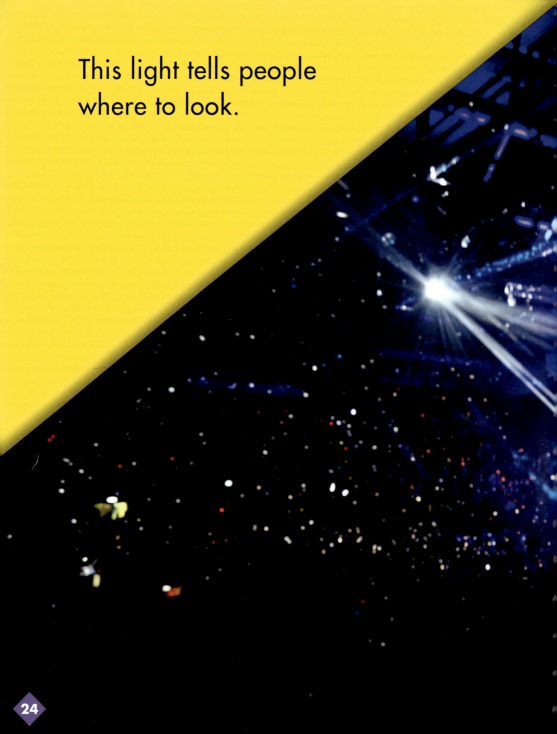

This light tells people
where to look.

This fish uses light to trick other fish into coming closer so it can eat them!

How have you used light today?

Some things make their own light.

Some things do not make their own light.

Light can pass through some materials but not others.

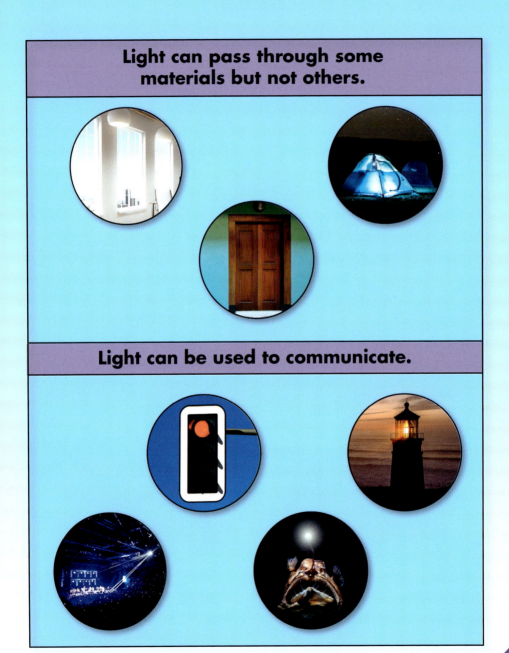

Light can be used to communicate.

CONNECTING CONCEPTS

CLOSE READING OF NONFICTION TEXT

Close reading helps children comprehend text. It includes reading a text, discussing it with others, and answering questions about it. Use these questions to discuss this book with your child:

- What causes the sun to create light?
- What is one thing that gives off its own light?
- Explain the meaning of *luminous*.
- How can a flashlight be both luminous and nonluminous?
- Why might you want to use an opaque curtain on your bedroom window?
- If the sky is dark, how can light from the sun make the moon visible in the sky?

SCIENCE IN THE REAL WORLD

With your child, walk around your house and make note of the sources of light in each room. Talk about which objects are luminous or nonluminous, and find examples of transparent, translucent, and opaque materials. Where light is blocked, identify the opaque material blocking the light.

SCIENCE AND ACADEMIC LANGUAGE

Make sure your child understands the meaning of the following words:

energy	gases	glow sticks	luminous	reflects	shine	nonluminous
waves	transparent	materials	translucent	opaque	communicate	trick

Have him or her use the words in a sentence.

FLUENCY

Fluency is the ability to read accurately with speed and expression. Help your child practice fluency by using one or more of the following activities:

1. Reread the book to your child at least two times while he or she uses a finger to track each word as it is read.
2. Read a line of the book, then reread it as your child reads along with you.
3. Ask your child to go back through the book and read the words he or she knows.
4. Have your child practice reading the book several times to improve accuracy, rate, and expression.

FOR FURTHER INFORMATION

Books:

Beck, W.H. *Glow: Animals with Their Own Night Lights*. New York, NY: HMH Books for Young Readers, 2015.

Johnson, Robin. *What Are Light Waves?* New York, NY: Crabtree, 2014.

Pfeffer, Wendy. *Light Is All Around Us*. New York, NY: HarperCollins, 2015.

Websites:

Bitesize: Light

http://www.bbc.co.uk/bitesize/ks2/science/physical_processes/light/read/1/

PBS Kids: Wild Kratt's Firefly Flash

http://pbskids.org/wildkratts/games/firefly-flash/

PBS Learning Media: Sid the Science Kid, Let There Be Light Parts 1-7

http://tpt.pbslearningmedia.org/resource/47861fd4-683a-4924-b490-3d53055309af/47861fd4-683a-4924-b490-3d53055309af/

Word List

Light uses the 106 words listed below. *High-frequency* words are those words that are used most often in the English language. They are sometimes referred to as sight words because children need to learn to recognize them automatically when they read. *Content words* are any words specific to a particular topic. Regular practice reading these words will enhance your child's ability to read with greater fluency and comprehension.

High Frequency-Words

a	come(ing)	in	make(s)	people	their	too
all	do	into	many	see	them	us
also	eat	is	no	so	there	use(d, s)
and	from	it	of	some	these	we
are	has	its	off	something	things	when
around	have	let	on	tell(s)	this	where
away	help(s)	like	other	that	through	why
can	how	look	own	the	to	you

Content Words

animals	doesn't	fish	living	reflects	sun('s)	waves
book	don't	flashlight	luminous	sea	sunlight	wood
bulbs	easily	gases	materials	shine	that's	
burning	else	glass	moon	ships	today	
can't	energy	glow	moving	shore	translucent	
closer	fast	it's	mushrooms	sky	transparent	
communicate	fireflies	kind	nonluminous	stay	travel(s)	
dark	fireworks	light	opaque	sticks	trick	

About the Author

Mary Lindeen is a writer, editor, parent, and former elementary school teacher. She has written more than 100 books for children and edited many more. She specializes in early literacy instruction and books for young readers, especially nonfiction.

About the Advisor

Dr. Shannon Cannon is an elementary school teacher in Sacramento, California. She has served as a teacher educator in the School of Education at UC Davis, where she also earned her Ph.D. in Language, Literacy, and Culture. As a member of the clinical faculty, she supervised pre-service teachers and taught elementary methods courses in reading, effective teaching, and teacher action research.